Action Sports

Horseback Riding

Gail B. Stewart

Capstone Press

MINNEAPOLIS

Printed in the United States of America.

Capstone Press • 2440 Fernbrook Lane • Minneapolis, MN 55447

Editorial Director   John Coughlan
Managing Editor   John Martin
Production Editor   James Stapleton
Copy Editor   Thomas Streissguth

Library of Congress Cataloging-in-Publication Data

Stewart, Gail, 1949-
    Horseback riding / by Gail B. Stewart.
      p. cm. -- (Action sports)
    Includes bibliographical references (p.) and index.
    ISBN 1-56065-263-2 $13.35
    1. Horsemanship--Juvenile literature. [1. Horsemanship.]
I. Title. II. Series.
SF309.2.S84 1996
798.2'3--dc20   95-5619
                                                    CIP
                                                    AC

99 98 97 96 95   6 5 4 3 2 1

Table of Contents

Chapter 1
Horseback Riding

Dana Warren is a 12-year-old girl in Alberta, Canada. She loves skiing, reading, and playing hockey with her three brothers. But there is only one thing that she's willing to get up every morning at 5:30 to do. That's horseback riding.

"Horseback riding is my number one love," Dana says. "I'm lucky. My family lives on a farm, and we have three horses. I can ride whenever I want. Even if I lived in town or in a big city, I think I'd find a way to ride as often as I could. It's the most fun in the world!"

Riding instructors show inexperienced riders how to control the horse.

"Horse Fever"

There are millions of people around the world who love horseback riding. Some are experienced riders who take part in horse shows and races. Others are happy just to take a horse for a trail ride on a sunny afternoon.

"Horse lovers come in all shapes and sizes," says one expert. "They are rich and poor, short and tall, boys and girls. The one thing they all share, though, is that bug we call 'horse fever.' That means they love being around horses, not just riding them. Horse lovers enjoy grooming them and feeding them, too. I've heard some people say they even like the smell of a horse barn. That's real horse fever!"

A Special Partnership

The love people have for horseback riding is nothing new. Since ancient times, people have enjoyed a special partnership with horses. Soldiers rode them in battle. Explorers crossed unknown lands on horseback. For centuries, people hunted for food on horseback.

Today, people do not depend on horses for hunting or fighting wars. They ride horses just for pleasure. But the partnership between people and horses is as strong as ever.

Chapter 2
Getting Started

Anyone who wants to ride horseback has many things to learn. "It is not just climbing onto a horse's back and galloping away," says one riding teacher. "Horses aren't like cars or bicycles. They are living, breathing animals with feelings and needs. You can't be a good rider without learning about these things."

Where Do You Start?

A good place to start is a riding school. Riding schools teach students at many levels. Some are nervous beginners who are still learning how to mount a horse. Others are

confident riders who want to learn to jump. Riding schools are often listed with local riding associations. You can also get information from the 4-H program of county extension offices and the organizations listed in the back of this book.

Good riding schools have clean stables and up-to-date equipment. Most schools have trails or outdoor arenas where horses and riders can practice. Many have indoor arenas, too. This is especially important in places where there is a lot of rain or snow.

Experts say that good teachers are the most important part of a riding school. "A good teacher puts a beginner at ease," says one riding school director. "The teacher's job is to match a new rider with a patient horse."

Marcie, a 14-year-old, agrees. "My riding teacher says that a green horse and a green rider don't mix. If both you and your horse are new to riding, things won't be easy. One of you has to know what to do."

What Riders Wear

Many beginning riders make the mistake of thinking they need lots of special riding clothes. You can buy expensive boots, jackets, riding pants, and hats, of course. But that isn't necessary. The only riders who need formal riding outfits are those who compete in horse shows.

A Helmet for Safety

For a beginner, safety is the guiding rule in choosing riding clothes. A helmet is essential. In fact, most riding schools will not let a rider mount a horse without a hard hat of some kind. Some hard hats are covered in fancy velvet. A hard hat like those worn by bicyclists is fine. It's a long way to the ground from the top of a horse. A helmet can protect a rider's head in case of a fall.

A good helmet—whether made of simple plastic or fancy velvet—is a must for riding safely.

Long Pants

Long pants are important, too. Wearing shorts when riding a horse will bring sores and saddle burns on the tender inner part of your leg. Many riders wear pants called **jodhpurs**. These are tight-fitting pants with padding on the inside of the leg. A comfortable pair of blue jeans, however, will also work.

Boots

It is not necessary to invest in an expensive pair of riding boots. Any boot or shoe with a heel will work. Experts say that a heel is absolutely necessary. Without it, a rider's foot might slip through the stirrup. A rider who falls can be dragged by the horse if her foot is caught in such a way.

Chapter 3

What the Horses Wear

Over the centuries, riders have developed equipment that makes riding horses easier and safer. This equipment, called tack, is worn by the horse. It is just as important as the special clothing worn by the rider.

The Saddle

The largest piece of tack is the saddle. This is the leather seat that is placed on the horse's back. A saddle keeps the rider securely on the horse. It has **stirrups** into which a rider places

A rider carefully places a saddle on his horse's back before heading for the trail.

her feet. When a saddle is used, riding is more comfortable for both the rider and the horse.

There are two basic kinds of saddles for riding. These are the Western saddle and the English saddle. The Western saddle is designed for cowboys who spend many long hours working on horseback. Its deep seat makes it more comfortable than other saddles. The front part, or **pommel**, is high. This makes it easy for a cowboy to loop a lariat around it when he is roping steers.

The English saddle is the most commonly used. It will most likely be the one a new rider will use. The English saddle is smaller than a Western saddle, and it has a lower pommel. It is lighter and less tiring to a horse. Both the Western saddle and the English saddle are attached to the horse by the girth–leather straps that pass under the horse's belly.

The Bridle

The **bridle** is a piece of tack that fits on the horse's head and in its mouth. It is made up of straps and metal pieces. The straps of a bridle

There are many different kinds of saddles, bridles, bits, and reins. This riding equipment is also known as tack.

are leather. The rider uses the bridle, with the **reins** attached to it, to control a horse.

Bits

A **bit** is a metal piece that fits inside the horse's mouth. When a rider pulls on the reins, the bit pulls against the horse's mouth. A horse

learns that by following the rider's demands, he can avoid the painful pressure of the bit.

There are many kinds of bits. One expert says there are more than 2,000 different styles. Many have strange names, like Straight Mouth Weymouth, German Hollow Mouth Snaffle, and Mullen Mouth.

The kind of bit a rider uses depends a lot on the kind of horse she rides. A horse that is stubborn or difficult to handle may need a severe bit. A severe bit is one that puts more pressure on the sensitive tissues of the horse's mouth.

The Snaffle Bit

A horse that is easy to handle may need only a **Snaffle bit**. This is a bit that is hinged in the middle. When the reins are pulled, the middle of the Snaffle bit bends. The horse feels pressure only in the corners of his mouth.

A close check of the horseshoes can prevent riding problems and serious injuries to the horse.

Rodeo cowboys need good, strong bits, like the Curb bit, to keep their horses under control in tough conditions.

"We put a Snaffle bit on a horse with a particularly tender mouth," explains one riding instructor. "We also use a Snaffle bit when the rider is inexperienced. New riders sometimes jerk and pull on the reins. That can hurt a horse's mouth. A gentler bit helps a lot."

The Curb Bit

There are times, however, when a more severe bit, like a **Curb bit**, is needed. A Curb bit is a solid piece of steel. It puts pressure on the top of the horse's mouth and on the areas between his front and back teeth.

Cowboys who herd cattle need full control for stopping and turning. They use a Curb bit. A Curb bit is also helpful when the horse is difficult to manage. Beginning riders almost never use a Curb bit.

"The important thing is to give the rider the greatest control possible, with the least amount of discomfort for the horse," says one expert.

Chapter 4

Learning to Ride

The rider is properly dressed. The horse is saddled and bridled. Now, the rider has to get on the horse. And there is more to mounting a horse than you may think.

Mounting

It is important to be quiet and gentle when you approach the horse. Quick, jerky movements and loud noises will frighten him. This makes him more difficult to mount.

It is also important to approach the horse from the left side. Horses are almost always mounted from the left side. It is what they are accustomed to. No one is sure how that custom began. Some historians think it began in the days when soldiers wore long swords on their left sides. It would have been impossible for them to mount from the right side. They would have had to swing their left leg, with the sword, over the horse.

"I always tell a beginner to grasp the reins in her left hand," says one riding instructor. "She should get hold of the pommel with the

All riders mount from the left side.

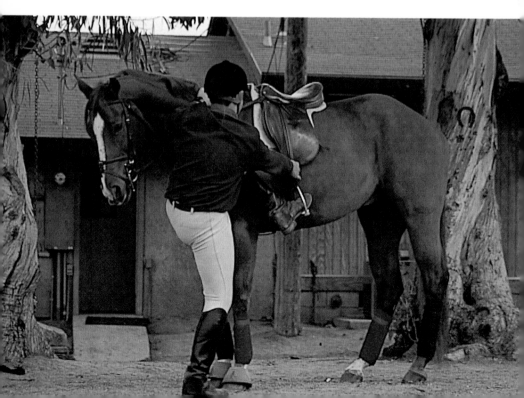

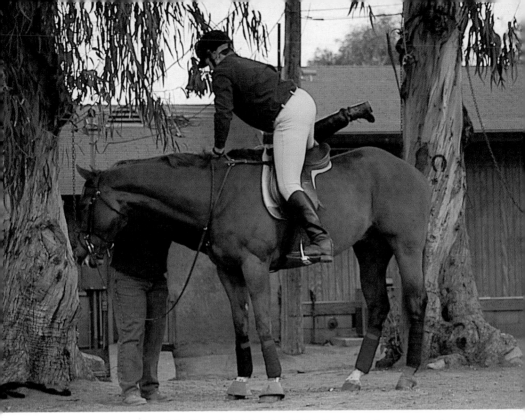

A gentle push with the right foot will help you rise up and over the horse's back.

same hand. Next, she should put her left foot in the stirrup and gently push with her right leg. In this way, she can swing her right leg over the horse."

It is important not to land heavily on the horse's back. That may startle him or cause him pain. Once the rider is on the horse, she should keep hold of the reins with both hands, sit up straight, and relax.

Using the Aids

Once the rider is mounted on the horse, she can start riding. But how does a horse know what the rider expects? How does he know when to turn or when to stop?

Riding instructors show beginners how to use **aids**, or cues, to signal their horses. A rider's voice is an aid, and so are her hands and her legs. Advanced riders can even signal their horses by simply shifting their weight from one part of the saddle to another.

A well-trained horse knows that when a rider squeezes her legs against his sides, he is supposed to move. A nudge on the left side will tell a horse to move right. Pushing lightly on his right side tells him to go left.

A rider has to know her horse very well in order to compete in horse shows.

The Reins

The reins are an important aid. Horses are trained to move in the direction of a rider's hands. This means that if a rider wants her horse to move left, a gentle pull on the left rein is a good signal. To stop, a rider pulls on both reins. This keeps the horse from moving his head forward.

The Rider's Voice

A rider's gentle voice can be a useful aid. Many beginners have a wrong impression of the voice aids they hear in cowboy movies. "Giddyap" and "Whoa" don't mean anything to a horse unless he has been trained to follow those signals. Experts say that yelling something at a horse can be dangerous. It can frighten the animal.

With a gentle word and firm control of the reins, a skilled rider guides her horse over a jump.

One instructor says: "The rider who yells 'Giddyap!' to a standing horse to get him to move might just take off a lot faster than she expects."

The Walk and the Trot

A horse has three **gaits**, or paces. The first is the walk. The second is called the **trot**. It is a little faster and quite a bit bumpier than the walk. The trot may feel uncomfortable at first

A good set of brushes and other supplies are necessary for grooming a horse.

One of the best parts of horseback riding is making friends with a beautiful animal.

because it may be difficult for a rider to keep her seat in the saddle.

Posting

A riding instructor can teach a rider how to **post**. A rider posts by lightly pushing down on the stirrups and then coming down into the saddle again. Done in rhythm, posting makes it

possible for the rider to move smoothly with the horse.

The Gallop and the Canter

The **gallop** is the third and fastest gait. It is a comfortable stride for the rider. There is no bouncing in and out of the saddle. A slower gallop is called a **canter**. It is just as comfortable as the gallop. Riding instructors do not let their students gallop or canter until they feel balanced and secure on their horses.

Experts say that, with practice, a rider can quickly master all of the horse's gaits. "Once you feel comfortable on the horse, the ride becomes exciting," says one horse lover. "You feel as though you're part of the horse. You feel as though you and the horse are moving together as a team."

In a jump, the timing has to be perfect. The judges are watching you carefully!

Chapter 5

The Dreams of a Young Rider

For some riders, horseback riding is so exciting that they have dreams of competing in riding events.

"I love to ride," says 12-year-old Joshua. "I wasn't sure I was going to like it at first. It was a little scary being on a tall horse. But I've been taking lessons for a year, and I'm more confident now. Someday I'd like to be in the jumping events of the Olympics."

Owning a Horse

There are some riders who think they want to own their horses. Horse experts encourage young people to have such dreams. But they say it is important to be practical, too.

"Owning a horse can be a wonderful experience," says one riding expert. "The rider who has the opportunity to own her own horse is very lucky. But it's a big commitment. And it's expensive. It costs money to buy a horse. And boarding a horse and feeding it are very expensive, too."

Helping around Riding Schools and Stables

There are other ways to be close to horses. Many riding schools and stables welcome young people as helpers. "I love it when my riding students are serious enough to want to help around the stable," says one teacher. "Horses need to be exercised, fed, and watered. Stalls need to be cleaned. Tack has to be polished. And, believe me, the horses love the attention!"

Reading about Riding

Many horse lovers enjoy reading books and magazines about horses and riding. "I like to learn about the different breeds, and their histories," says one 11-year-old rider. "I like Appaloosas the best."

Librarians and booksellers are often able to direct young readers to good books about horses and riding. Some of the best writers about horses are Walter Farley, Marguerite Henry, and Bonnie Bryant.

Glossary

aids–cues or signals a rider gives to her horse

bit–a metal piece that fits inside the horse's mouth

bridle–a series of straps and buckles that fits over the horse's head

canter–a slow gallop

Curb bit–a severe bit used for hard-to-manage horses

gait–a pace at which the horse moves

gallop–one of a horse's fastest paces

jodhpurs–tight-fitting riding pants with protective padding in the legs

pommel–the raised part of a saddle that sits in front of the rider

posting–a rider's rhythmic up-and-down movement in the saddle when her horse trots

reins–the bridle's leather straps held by a rider

Snaffle bit–a gentle bit used for beginning riders, and on horses with sensitive mouths

stirrup–the loops of the saddle through which the rider puts her feet

trot–a gait faster than a walk, but slower than a canter. A trot feels bumpy to inexperienced riders.

To Learn More

Bryant, Bonnie. *Horse Crazy.* New York: Bantam, 1988.

Clemens, Virginia Phelps. *A Horse of Your Own: A First-Time Owner's Primer of Horse Keeping.* New York: Prentice Hall, 1991.

Edwards, Elwyn Hartley. *The Ultimate Horse Book.* New York: Dorling Kindersley, 1991.

Farley, Walter. *The Black Stallion.* New York: Random House, 1941.

Henry, Marguerite. *Album of Horses.* Chicago: Rand McNally, 1951.

Henry, Marguerite. *Misty of Chincoteague.* Chicago: Rand McNally, 1947.

Rodenas, Paula. *The Random House Book of Horses and Horsemanship.* New York: Random House, 1991.

Stewart, Gail B. *The Appaloosa Horse.* Minneapolis: Capstone Press, 1995.

_____. *The Arabian Horse.* Minneapolis: Capstone Press, 1995.

_____. *The Quarter Horse.* Minneapolis: Capstone Press, 1995.

_____. *The Thoroughbred Horse.* Minneapolis: Capstone Press, 1995.

Some Useful Addresses

American Horse Shows Association
220 E. 42nd Street, Suite 409
New York, NY 10017-5876

Canadian Equestrian Federation/Federation equestre canadienne
1600 James Naismith Drive, Suite 501
Gloucester ON K1B 5N4
Canada

Association for Horsemanship Safety and Education
5318 Old Bullard Road
Tyler, TX 75703

American Horse Council
1700 K St., NW, Suite 300
Washington, DC 20006

The North American Riding Association for the Handicapped
P.O. Box 33150
Denver, CO 80233

Index